MW00862175

# MEL BAY PRESENTS

# SOLO JAZZ GUITAR-II

## by ALAN de MAUSE

### Graded Solos for Players at All Levels

**A stereo cassette tape of the music in this book is now available. The publisher strongly recommends the use of this cassette tape along with the text to insure accuracy of interpretation and ease in learning.**

# Foreword

This book contains outstanding jazz guitar arrangements in the style of many of today's legendary performers. Alan de Mause has done a masterful job in his arrangements and original compositions in capturing the beauty and diversity found in jazz guitar. Other Alan de Mause books published by Mel Bay Publications are: *Art of Solo Jazz Guitar Vol. I, 101 Jazz Guitar Licks, Jazz Guitar Etudes,* and *Jazz Guitar Handbook.* In addition, Alan transcribed *Joe Pass Virtuoso III.* A companion stereo cassette is available with this book and is highly recommended. It is our pleasure to present yet another book in the fine Alan de Mause Jazz Guitar Series.

## From the author

Thanks for making my original *Solo Jazz Guitar* a personal best hit. Your notes and comments about it have been invaluable to me. In fact, I have based this book on your requests, which were—

*All levels of solos.* Easy, intermediate, and advanced. If you are a near-beginner, you can start with this book and later move on to *Solo Jazz Guitar.*

*Shorter* pieces. So that you can learn them in less time and build a repertory of pieces more quickly.

*More flat pick arrangements.* Much of this material can be played with a flat pick or fingerstyle.

*Guitar accompaniment arrangements.* You can put the same care into accompanying singers and other guitarists as you do when soloing.

*A piece for 7-string guitar.* For the lunatic fringe among you, including me.

## About the author

Guitarist Alan de Mause lives in New York, where he performs, authors music instruction books, teaches both at Columbia University and his studio where he develops his *GUITAR POWER!* correspondence study course materials for students around the world.

When not involved in music, Alan does computer consulting and software applications teaching. Using computer-aided music sequencing and music graphics software, he provides services for musicians, such as arranging, lead sheets, flyers, posters, and other promotional materials.

He invites you to let him know how you like this or any of his other books, by writing to him at *GUITAR POWER!*, 10 Jones Street 4H, New York City, New York, 10014.

## Acknowledgement:

—to my students, for tune testing.

## Thank you:

—to Christine Sotmary for helping me catch the typo's, write-o's and oh-oh's in the manuscript.
—to Marilyn Ries for editing the **master tape**.

# Alan de Mause

Photo by Michael Ian

# Table of Contents

# House Of The Rising Sun

**Traditional blues**

*The House of the Rising Sun,* like most solo guitar, consists of music in at least two parts. The upper part (note stems up) is most often the melody, and the lower part (note stems down), an accompanying bass. With fingerstyle technique, the melody is usually played with alternating index and middle fingers, rest stroke, and thumb plays the bass, free stroke.*

Another signature of solo guitar is the overlapping of notes. Some sustain and others move. Watch that the proper finger(s) do the same. Open string bass notes are easy. Note how the bass note helps determine the harmony and keep the rhythm going.

Pick or fingerstyle

slowly

*For more detailed information on right hand fingerstyle technique, see my **Solo Jazz Guitar,** or **Jazz Guitar Etudes.** Both are published by Mel Bay Publications, Inc.

# Simple Blues

AdM

In traditional blues the melody and bass take turns in a call-and-response dialogue. Since this is an old-timey blues, put a slight swing or shuffle feeling to it.

Pick or fingerstyle

medium

# Scarborough Faire

**Traditional**

In *Scarborough Faire,* arpeggios or drone tones are used to propel and fill out a slow moving melody. The melodic line switches from the lower note to the top note and back, and the thumb sometimes travels higher than usual, so watch the road map. Play the accented notes ( > ) louder so the basic melody will emerge.

Fingerstyle

Slow-medium

# Flambreau

AdM

*Flambreau* must be played with fingerstyle technique. Unlike the first three pieces, there are many instances of melody notes being played *simultaneously* with bass notes which lie more than two strings away. This can only be achieved using two fingers, or finger and thumb. To play melody and bass together, use a rest stroke with the fingers and a free stroke with the thumb. The only exception is in the fourth phrase, measures 13 - 16, where you should fingerpick with free strokes to allow the arpeggios to ring together.

This is a jazz flavored piece based on the flamence dance form, *Soleares*. This form typically has a four-measure phrase cycle. Give it your best Spanish *angst*. Picking near the bridge helps. If you like *Flambreau,* there is a more advanced similar piece, *Solears Jazz Waltz,* in my Mel Bay Book, **Solo Jazz Guitar.**

Fingerstyle

# Saint Jim's Clinic

AdM

There are simultaneous, independent rhythms in the melody and bass lines of *Saint Jim's Clinic*. This interplay of sustaining and moving notes gives the effect of two instruments being played. It's also more challenging to play. Watch the overlapping notes and finger accordingly. The two angled brackets in measure one and five indicate where to begin a full barre.

Fingerstyle

slow-medium

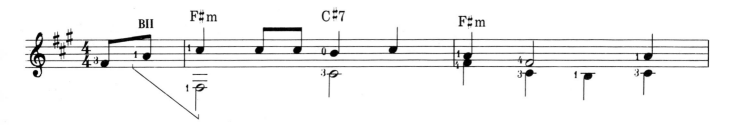

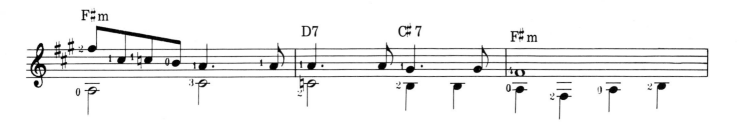

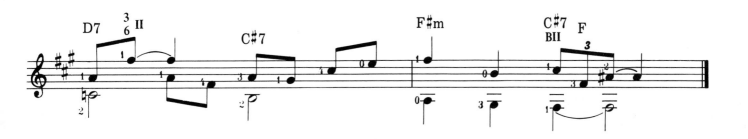

# A Pretty

AdM

Accent the first beat slightly to indicate that you are playing a waltz. While *A Pretty* isn't crammed full of notes, it has three independent overlapping voices. So stay on your toes. Waltz with it.

Fingerstyle
medium

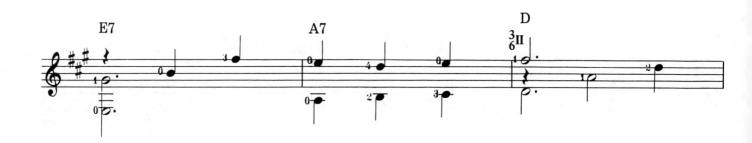

# Eight Of Rhythm

AdM

*Eight of Rhythm* is the first hard core bebop line in this book, so give it your jazziest interpretation. For starters, listen to the optional accompanying cassette for my interpretation. It includes techniques used earlier: melody on top with bass notes accompanying, melody in the bass with accompaniment on top, parts played alternately and together. The piece is an improvisation on the first eight measures of George Gershwin's jazz classic, *I've Got Rhythm.*

Fingerstyle
medium Bebop

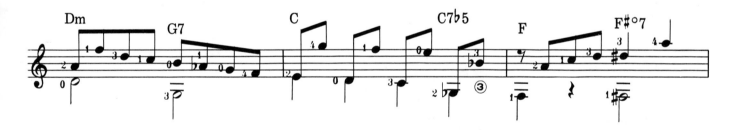

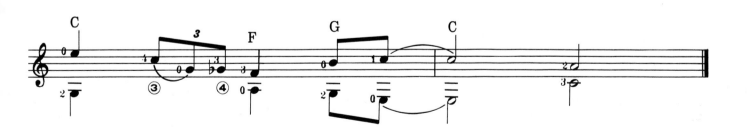

# Ticklefingers

AdM

*Ticklefingers* is a minor blues. Here is a chance to work on the fluidity of your fingerstyle index-middle combination in playing longer jazz melodic lines. Aim for seamless phrases. Try skimming along the plane of the strings (rest stroke) with fingernails *only* so that you don't get stuck between them.

Fingerstyle

medium-fast Bebop

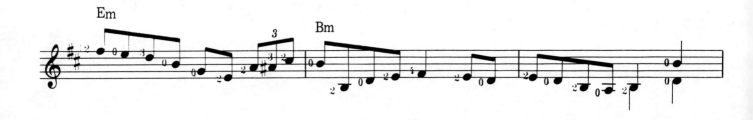

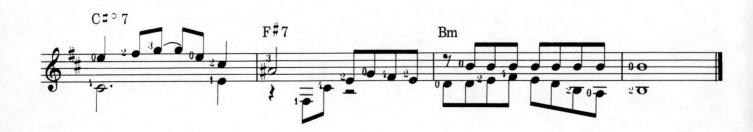

# An Ok Place To Be

AdM

This is the first tune incorporating three note chords.  Often the lowest note is a tenth below the melody and the inner note is a fourth, fifth, or sixth below the melody.  Since chords can't be played with rest strokes, use a firm, loud free stroke — especially on the top melody note of the chords.

Fingerstyle

medium

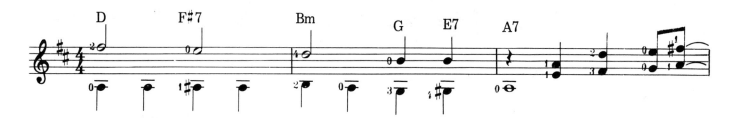

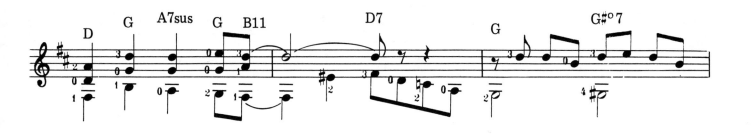

# Two Views Of Blues

AdM

*Two Views of Blues* illustrates the simple but important idea of using *contrast* between a melody and a bass line. In the first chorus, the bass is moving slowly, while the melody is more active. When the second chorus starts, the bass shifts into four-to-the-bar walking thumb bass style accompaniment, and the melody is slower, rhythmically. You can also use both techniques within a single chorus, of course.

Fingerstyle

medium

14

# Gypsy Jazz Eyes

AdM

This reworking of the *Dark Eyes* has the flavor of traditional jazz violinists approach to improvisation. The original melody is kept, and a cadenza - like improvisation occurs in the spots normally occupied by held notes.

Pick or fingerstyle

*rubato*, with forward motion

# The Bad Girl

AdM
traditional blues

The *Bad Girl* starts quietly with a one note melody ascending to the higher area of the neck. Then it gathers a close voiced descending line, changing to open-voiced three note chords. It builds to a climax and a full stop, after which it ends quietly. still descending in the bass line, to a climax and a full stop. A short quiet ending follows. Give this sad, lovely, bluesy traditional folk song a some poignancy as you can. It deserves it. It's one of my personal favorites in this collection.

* Brief full stop

16

# The Following Solos Are For The More Advanced Guitarist

# Be Good, Lady

AdM

Solos needn't be crammed to the corners with extended chords and simultaneous multi-rhythmic lines.
Instead, the same effects can be implied with fewer tools used skillfully. *Be Good, Lady*, based on the
similar chord progressions of *Oh! Lady Be Good* (George Gerswhin) is "only" a single line improvisation. Let some notes ring for a nice effect.

This style can easily be played with a pick.

Pick or fingerstyle

medium but freely

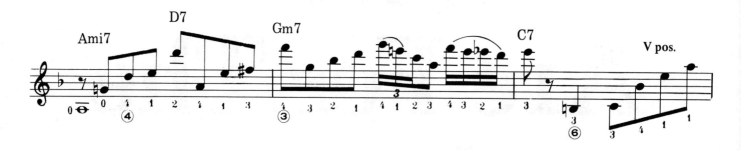

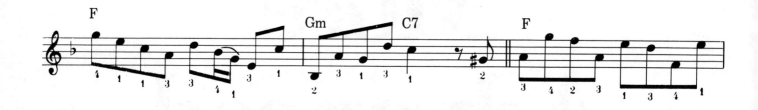

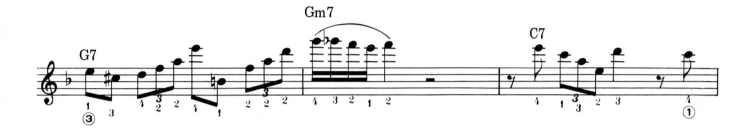

19

# My Laughing Love

AdM

Good solo guitarists have the technique and the musical understanding to create better than average accompaniment for singers and instrumentalists. *My Laughing Love* is a single line accompaniment based on similar chord changes to *My Funny Valentine,* by Rodgers and Hart. Since this accompaniment is in the lower range, you may like to interpret it as a line played by a bass player. However, this is not mandatory. A line is a line, and it can work just as well if you move it up an octave and think of yourself as a flute player. Or even play it as is, and think of yourself as a guitarist. . .

Pick or fingerstyle

medium

# Corpus Et Spiritus

AdM

In this accompaniment arrangement there is a variety of musical components — arpeggios, chords, runs, rhythmic changes, extended harmony. The primary device on which all of the above hangs is the leading bass note on the first and third beats of every measure. This technique works best backing singers or instrumentalists who like the accompanist to lead, rather than follow them.

*Corpus et Spiritus* is an accompaniment based on harmony very similar to the chord changes of *Body and Soul* (Heyman, Sour, Eyton and Green).

Fingerstyle

Rubato, picking up to a walking tempo

# Are You All The Things?

AdM

Like *Be Good, Lady, Are You All the Things?* is sparse in terms of notes per measure, but is nonetheless very active musically. One device used here, starting with measure one, is the very active lower line melody played against a sustaining upper melody note. Don't skimp on quality of sound for either line. Monitor each one, one ear apiece . . .

In the middle section there are several measures using walking tenths (a jazz piano technique) as an accompanying device to the melody.

Fingerstyle

medium rubato with forward motion

24

# Blues For Phyllis

AdM

This blues consists of a theme and two improvised choruses. I intended the whole piece to be reminiscent of electric piano style in the bebop mode: even, flowing eighth notes over sparse comping or single note bass. Notice that the harmony of the second improvised chorus switches from standard blues to an alternate bebop progression. Don't forget to use your rest stroke in the melody to create the punchy nuances of bebop. Listen to the tape.

Fingerstyle
medium

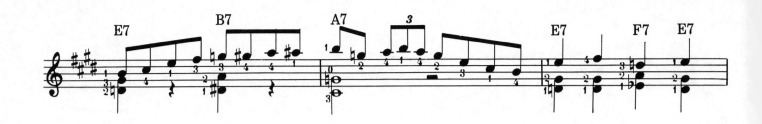

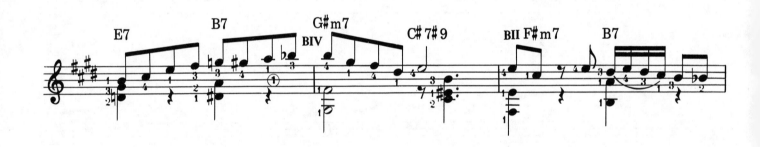

# The Following Selection My Fling Is For Seven String Players

(On the cassette an extra ending is added.)

# My Fling

AdM

Okay, seven string players, this one is for you. Also, you normal folks can play this if you move the notes marked with a circled "7" to an octave higher on the fifth string. This improvisation on similar changes to *My Romance* (Rogers and Hart) is less the hard side of jazz and more the romantic. On the cassette (only) there is an extra ending added as a referential nod of thanks to the Daddy of all seven string players, George Van Eps.

Fingerstyle

slow rubato, but moving forward

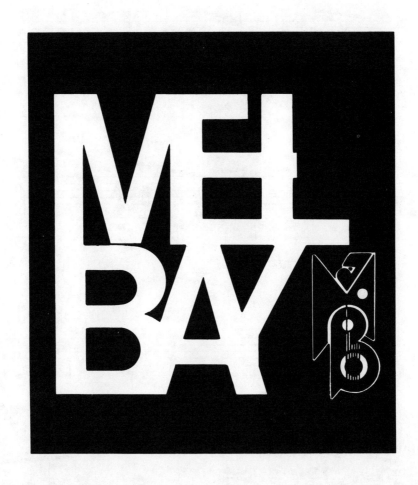

Great Music at Your Fingertips